MASS:

7 Secrets To Build Muscle Fast As Hell

By Brandon Carter

www.BrandonCarter.com

Disclaimer & Copyright

This book is not intended as a substitute for the medical advice of physicians. The reader should regularly consult a physician in matters relating to his/her health and particularly with respect to any symptoms that may require diagnosis or medical attention.

The information provided in this book is designed to provide helpful information on the subjects discussed. This book is not meant to be used, nor should it be used, to diagnose or treat any medical condition. For diagnosis or treatment of any medical problem, consult your own physician. The publisher and author are not responsible for any specific health or allergy needs that may require medical supervision and are not liable for any damages or negative consequences from any treatment, action, application or preparation, to any person reading or following the information in this book. References are provided for informational purposes only and do not constitute endorsement of any websites or other sources. Readers should be aware that the websites listed in this book may change.

Bro Laboratories
480 6th Avenue #219
New York, NY 10011
www.BroLaboratories.com

Table Of Contents

About The Author

My Name is Brandon Carter. I have been a personal trainer and nutritionist for over 10 years at some of the top gyms in New York City. I have worked as a fitness model for Nike, Adidas, Puma, Brand "Jordan" and more. I have been featured in and on the cover of multiple fitness magazines. I have also trained professional athletes and fitness models.

My goal is to help as many people as possible reach their fitness goals. My blog (http://www.brandoncarter.com/) has helped hundreds of people do just that. Here are a few testimonials:

Testimonials

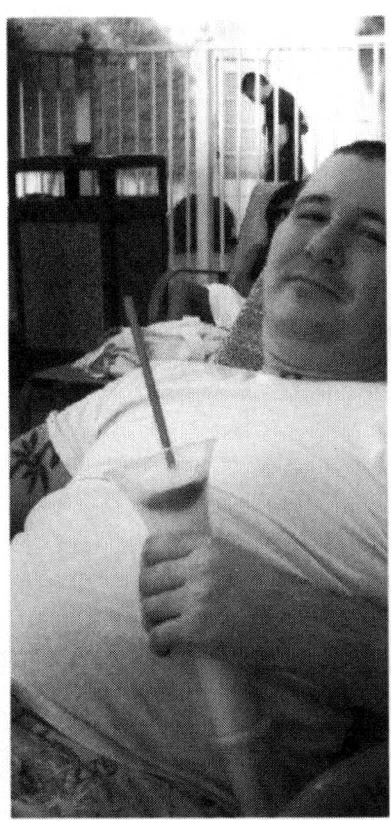

(Some people questioned the authenticity of this pic when I first posted it because his tattoo is on the other arm in the second pic. It is because he took the pic in the mirror. I don't want to get into the "science" of that, but if I take a pic of my reflection, my tattoos switch sides too. Like magic!)

"All of my coworkers, family and friends ask me how I lost all my weight (currently at a loss of 58 lbs) and built all of my muscle. I tell them that I used all that I learned from you as a base of my eating habits and workout plans. I wanted to thank you for all the helpful information and I wanted to send you a before and current (2 months ago) picture of myself so you can see my progress thanks to you. The before picture was a little over 1 year from the more current picture. I hope Brandon himself gets to see this because I would like him to know the huge impact his words and videos have had on my life and hopefully many others."
-Michael Alexander

"I watched your youtube videos, which helped me with my body transformation. Check out my weight loss album!"
- Kamari

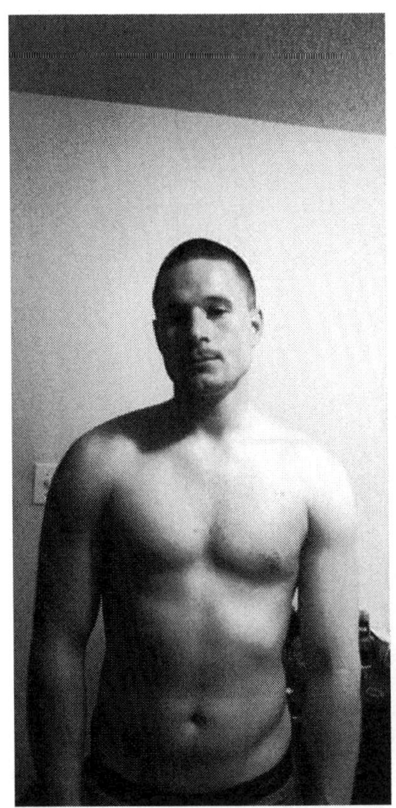

"Results don't just come over night, and supplements can only do so much... But these workouts Brandon provides are the real deal! For real results and real motivation quit doing the same workouts and try something new! I did, and I'm seeing satisfying results already!!"

- Joshua Everett

"I'd like to thank you for everything you've done up til now. Thanks to you I was able to accomplish my FItness Goals in the past year. Here are 2 pics. Sorry for the before pic found no better one.Would be glad to see it on your Facebook site or homepage so that I can also motivate others to not give up best regards!"
- Christopher Scharner

"Hi Brandon, my name is Ergin YALI and I'm currently 17 years old. First of all I want to thank you for all the great and helpful information that I learnt from you and from your site. Most fitness instructors, and nutritionists I have talked at the past made me keep wasting my time and money, but you man, you are completely different. I learned almost all my eating and workout plans/tips from you.

Thanks again for sharing all your knowledge with me and others. Till 9 months ago I was 105 kg, now I m currently 70 kg. My waist reduced 143cm to 86 cm. No other words needed, photos describe my situation. I got leaner and also added a lot of muscle. I hope you get this mail man, because I would like you to know your words, tips, inspirational quotes and videos changed my life. I hope others can reach their goals too. Also you're a brilliant musician man, KEEP IT UP!!! (sorry for wrong sentences man, my english is not that great)."

- Ergin Yali

See more testimonials on my blog: http://www.brandoncarter.com/

I believe you can achieve results like the ones above and even better! I am living proof that these 7 secrets work for anyone who applies them. I've learned through experimentation and application that these are the best and fastest proven ways to achieve your best body. It would be selfish to keep these secrets to myself so I'm sharing them all in this book. I hope they change your life like they have changed mine. Lets get to work!

Brandon Carter

Fitness Blog http://www.brandoncarter.com/
YouTube http://www.youtube.com/HighLifeWorkout
Facebook https://www.facebook.com/BigBrandonCarter
Twitter https://twitter.com/BCarterMusic
Instagram http://instagram.com/bcartermusic
SnapChat: @KillerCarter187

WARNING: READ THIS BEFORE YOU GO ANY FURTHER!

In an effort to keep this book short, I have links to videos and blog posts that explain some of the topics in greater detail. Be sure to click on them if you need more clarity on a topic or if you want to see my video making skills.

I use foul language when I talk. My last book, *Ultimate Cuts: Seven Secrets To Burn Fat Fast As Hell* was a number one Amazon bestseller and has hundreds of five-star reviews. The only complaints came from people who did not like the foul language in the video links. I find it odd that someone would buy a book with the word "Hell" in the title then complain about any foul language. I deliberately put that word in the title to discourage more conservative people from buying it, KNOWING they would end up focusing on the wrong details. "Never criticize, condemn, or complain" said Dale Carnegie in his best selling self-help book, *How To Win Friends And Influence People.* Having that said, read that book first if you haven't yet done so, and ***if foul language offends you, please do not watch the videos. Thank you.***

To View The Bar Code Boxes, Download A "QR Code Scanner" On Your Smartphone To Scan And View The Links In The Following Pages... Enjoy!

Introduction To Mass

For the bulk of my career I never wanted to be a really "big" guy. I was more interested in being athletic and lean, so I never went out of my way to put on a tremendous amount of muscle mass. It just wasn't my primary goal. I have helped others achieve tremendous amounts of muscle but I never wanted that for myself. In 2013 however, all of that changed.

For whatever reason in 2013, I decided that I wanted to become a lot bigger and a lot stronger.
During that time I put on about 10 pounds.

Many of you may be thinking that 10 pounds is not a significant gain during a 12 month period. But you have to remember that I did it while gaining between very little and NO FAT. It was all quality weight - 10 pounds of solid muscle! Anybody can add muscle *and* fat to quickly gain 10 pounds but to add 10 pounds of Herculean is difficult. Especially because I have been training for so long. When you have been training for over 10 years, putting on muscle is a lot harder than when you first start. If you are a beginner or in your first few years of training, then you should be able to accomplish even more impressive results than I did in that same period of time.

I was able to accomplish my results using the exact techniques that I am sharing with you in this book. In the following chapters you will learn:

- How to build lean muscle mass without gaining fat
- The quickest ways to burn body fat
- How to become more disciplined in the gym and in life
- How to become more confident
- What the best exercises are for putting on muscle MASS
- How to spend less time in the gym and build MORE muscle
- The best diet plan to build muscle mass
- How to naturally increase your testosterone levels
- Plus much more!

The benefits of following the right exercise and diet program are vast, starting with the discipline required to stay consistent and ending with an increased total well being; Not to mention your improved body composition, and a great confidence boost.

The number one reason to train with resistance and pump iron is the acquisition of physical strength and muscle mass. Physical strength is a sort of crux connected to what it means to be a man. Without actual physical strength, men aren't all of that different from their female counterparts. And while there are several other virtues connected with masculinity, like decisiveness along with mental fortitude, many stem from your physical embodiment of strength.

Size Matters

Once you gain a significant amount of muscle mass you'll notice that people start to treat you differently and your interactions with other humans, both male and female, will change drastically.

I grew up on the Southside of Chicago. To say it is a "rough area" would be a gross understatement. I used to get in a lot of fights, I used to get robbed, and would frequently be intimidated by gangbangers.

Initially, I began lifting weights as a way to defend myself against potential evil-doers. But the interesting thing that happened once I gained size - people just stopped messing with me. I made myself a harder (and more intimidating) target.

I call this the "*Lion in The Room*" philosophy. If you walk into a room and you see a lion, you're probably not going to mess with it. Even if he is just sleeping and being non-aggressive you still have to be cautious of him. Even if you are a bigger stronger lion, you still are going to think twice about fighting another lion. There is a reason that predators hunt prey or those weaker and more vulnerable than themselves. Lions do not have a natural predator in the wild. And last time I checked, not too many people are eating (or messing with) them.

But not only did men stop wanting to fight me and steal my money, it seemed that once I built some size, more people wanted to be friends with me. It seemed that my size earned me more respect and a higher status in general amongst my peers.

In Robert Cialdini's best-selling book *Influence* he talks about this subject and how it works in the animal kingdom. "In some animal societies...size is an important factor in determining which animal would achieve a high level in the group."

News Flash: Women Like Muscular Men

Women also seemed to find me a lot more attractive as I became more muscular. Sure, there is a point of diminishing returns when it comes to muscles and being attractive to women. Yet still, from a strictly evolutionary perspective, women are most attracted to strong, healthy, muscular men.

In an article from *Psychology Today,* Vinita Mehta, Ph.D., Ed.M. explains:

> "Studies have revealed a not so obvious factor that explains why some women find themselves irresistibly drawn to masculine men. Quite simply, it's because they're healthier. And from an evolutionary perspective, good health has great value in the mating market because it increases the probability of reproductive success. Previous research shows that masculine features are associated with markers of healthfulness, including upper body strength, less oxidative stress, and fewer bouts of illness. In addition, elevated testosterone levels are linked to a powerful immune system response."

I think the vast majority of women who claim to not be "into" fit guys are really saying, "I am not hot or fit enough enough myself to attract the most alpha of men therefore I will preemptively disqualify them." **Being more muscular will make you more attractive, period**.

The problem is when anyone is TOO into his or her appearance, so much that other priorities are neglected. That is when it's a problem. Either way, when people with average physiques see a significantly more fit person it's easy to assume person is self-absorbed. Sometimes it's true, other times it's simply a rationalization for the average person's laziness and lack of drive.

If you can defy that stereotype by being well read, and well rounded, so it doesn't look like your life is all about your physique and not much else, than a more fit body will only further compliment you and will make you more attractive and desirable to the fairer sex.

Steroids!?

When people see me with 10 additional pounds of muscle I get accused of taking steroids (this is actually one of the best compliments an athlete can get haha). But if you look back at all my YouTube videos from the beginning of 2013 to now, you can see that I put on muscle at a very slow pace while maintaining extremely low body fat. I gained muscle at a rate of less than one pound per month. Steroids or any other performance-enhancing drugs work a lot better than that.

In fact, nothing works as well as steroids but I DO NOT recommend them. I have never used any steroids in my life. I'm not trying to knock anyone who has (Arnold Schwarzenegger is one of my idols) but my decision to not use steroids is based on the fact that steroids make your genitals shrink. I don't think any amount of muscle, money, or fame is worth putting your genitalia in harm's way, but this is just my humble opinion. If performance-enhancing drugs are something you are interested in then this is not the book for you, but you should check out a video from my friend Elliot Hulse about his experience with steroids before you embark on that journey. http://bit.ly/1trCcb6

Full disclosure: the only drugs I have ever experimented with are marijuana, LSD, and psychedelic mushrooms but that's a whole different story for a whole different book.

If you're ready to naturally put on as much muscle as your body can handle while staying as lean (and drug free) as possible, then let's dive right into the material.

Secret #1: Micro Bulking and Cutting

"If you are not willing to risk the unusual, you will have to settle for the ordinary."
-Jim Rohn

Nobody wants to get fat. That's why I am going to present a method of bulking up and building muscle that will allow you to increase muscle size without getting fat at the same time.

Traditional Bulking and Cutting

The human body is not good at building muscle and burning fat at the same time under normal circumstances. That's why traditional bulking programs suggest that you *bulk up* for up to six months at a time. FUCK THAT! That's half of the year! *The major problem with that is that when you bulk for that amount of time you also gain a lot of fat.* Then you are told to cut (the fat) for another six months. During those six months you lose the fat that you built up (assuming you're cutting properly) but you may also lose a lot of the muscle you built in the process. What a waste of time and energy! I've had roller coaster relationships; it's not as thrilling as the rides at Six Flags. And I don't want any kind of relationship like that with my own god damn body. After an entire year is up you HOPE that you have a net gain of muscle. But that's the main problem with traditional bulking programs - you look like SHIT for half the year. "Ain't nobody got time for that!"

I honestly don't even like the term "bulk" or "bulking" besides for the fact that it rhymes with "Hulk" or "Hulking". I love when words rhyme ...because I am black. It's quite apparent to me that many use the word "bulk" as an excuse that allows them to rationalize eating more and training less. Then they say "I don't look my best right now because I am bulking" or something of the like. Yea, yea. We believe you.

But alas, this is how professional bodybuilders train. They bulk up for half of the year and then cut up for the second half of the year in order to look like they do when you see them on stage flexing in man bikinis. In layman's terms they look like shit for half the year, then they only start to look good once they are well into the cutting phase. Professional bodybuilders may be able afford to look like shit for half of the year (a.k.a. the "off-season"), *because they only have to look good during contest season,* as far as their career goes. For guys like you and I however, **THERE IS NO "off-season" for our lives!** And life is too short to spend half of every year being a complete fat ass. All "jokes" aside, you can ruin your entire physique by getting fat during the bulking. That is because when you get fat and start to gain more fat cells, those cells never go away!

Fat Cells Never Go Away!?

I hope you're sitting down right now. What I'm about to say is going to scare the shit out of you. I was far into bodybuilding by the time I learned this and it's something I wish I had learned much earlier on. Here it is: *When you start gaining fat your fat cells grow. And once they grow to capacity, the cells split, or divide, now you have more fat cells than you started with. The problem with that is now you have set a new baseline for the amount of cells your body carries.* ***Your fat cells can grow and shrink but you will never lose them!***

So, once you have gained additional fat cells, from that point on - for the rest of your life, it will be easier for you to gain fat and more difficult to lose It. *That's why it's imperative that you do not gain fat while bulking.*

I know a lot of you are going to find that hard to believe, so I have provided a few sources to corroborate my statements.

"You are born with a set number of fat cells. If you eat more calories than your body needs, your fat cells stretch to store these extra calories as triglycerides. You may even gain new fat cells when the cells have enlarged to their maximum size. ***Once created, however, fat cells remain in your body forever; they may shrink in size when you lose weight, but they never go away*** " -Johns Hopkins University School Of Medicine

"Fat cells can shrink -- but they don't go away... even after the weight comes off, your number of fat cells stays the same, and it will be an uphill battle to keep the pounds off" - Dr. Sanjay Gupta

"Fat cells may shrink (or grow) in size, but not in number." -Louise Chang, MD (WebMD)

I will show you the method I use, for myself, and the people I train to gain muscle without gaining fat. This method may build muscle a bit slower than traditional bulk methods, but *it will prevent the production of new fat cells and keep you looking good year-round*. I believe that trade-off is worth it.

Micro Cutting And Bulking (MCAB)

You want to look good all year-round (while still building muscle mass). Instead of bulking for six months then trying to trim the fat off for the next six months, micro bulking and cutting (MCAB) consists of a bulking phase that lasts between two to four weeks, followed by a cutting phase that also lasts for two to four weeks.

Here's how it works - Before you even begin to try to build new muscle, you CUT and get as lean as you want to be before you start bulking. Ideally, you want to have a visible six pack before you start bulking. *If you start bulking before you are as lean as you want to be then you run the risk of creating additional fat cells.* And if you're kind of chubby now, then you start bulking, the multiplication of your fat cells and production of new ones is almost guaranteed.

So it is imperative that you get as lean as you want to be before you start the bulk. Once you are as lean as you want to be, ideally to the point where you have visible abs, then you start the bulk. *I highly suggest that when you're bulking, bulk only until your abs begin to fade. This will ensure that you are not bulking for too long and gaining too much fat, therefore reducing the possibility of you gaining additional fat cells during your bulk.*

Micro bulking and cutting also has many psychological benefits. When you are doing traditional bulking and cutting you kind of start to get tired of eating tons of food every day for six months. It sounds cool at first but after a month or two (or even as early as the first week) of being full all the time while force-feeding yourself, it starts to become an annoying chore. It can be literally dreadful.

Traditional cutting sucks. Do you really want to diet for six months? My answer is HELL NO! It's a lot easier to stay motivated during any diet if you know you only have to do it for a few weeks as opposed to a several months. Hence the psychological benefits of MCAB over non-MCAB. You start to look forward to cutting while you're bulking and vice versa.

How To Micro Cut

Remember when I said you want to get as lean as you want to be before you start the bulk? Well, for some of you that might take more than a micro cut. You might have to go on a full on traditional cut before you can bulk if you are already significantly overweight.

The last thing you want to do is bulk if you're already kind of fat because multiplying your current number of fat cells is the worst possible scenario. If you have a significant amount of fat to lose before you can see your abs, then I suggest you read my other book, "*Ultimate Cuts: Seven Secrets To Burn Fat Fast As Hell*".

http://amzn.to/1Ys82AI

"*Ultimate Cuts*" breaks down the fat burning process in great detail.

But this is not one of those books that tries to get you to buy other books, so I will go into the cutting process here. If you want, or need, more detail in advance then "*Ultimate Cuts*" is definitely worth checking out.

Cutting Basics

Cutting, or burning fat, is not as complex as most people think. It can actually be broken down into one sentence:

To lose fat, all you have to do is burn more calories than you consume.

When you are burning more calories than you consume you are in what is called "a caloric deficit."

Cardio, fat burning pills, dieting, fasting, etc., are all simply tactics to help your body get into a state of burning more calories than it consumes to put your body in a "caloric deficit".

Being in a "caloric deficit" is literally the only way to burn fat.

And the best way to get in a "caloric deficit" is adjusting your diet. Diet is way more effective than cardio when it comes to burning fat. In fact, you can actually burn fat without doing any exercise at all! For example, On average, running 1 mile burns about 100 calories. Sounds great right? Until you realize that there are about 100 calories in a fucking banana!

With that said, you can see how it's much easier to just eat less than it is to try to *burn* calories off. I am not trying to say that you should not do cardio, but I am trying to say that *you cannot out train a bad diet*.

I go over this concept more in this video: "How To Lose Weight Without Exercise"

http://bit.ly/28FziQw

I have worked in gyms that employed overweight aerobics teachers! This is a person whose job is literally doing cardio all day, but they are still overweight. How can that be? I'll tell you how, it's because his goofy ass is drinking 400 calorie Starbucks drinks multiple times a day then eating cakes and other sweet treats when he gets home to his Mommy's house!

So even while he is doing cardio all day he's still not losing any weight because he was not in a caloric deficit. You can do an "Insanity Workout" eight times a day and still not lose any weight if you are consuming more calories than you burn. That is because ***you cannot out train a bad diet***.

There are only three things in life that I know for sure:

1. Michael Jordan was the greatest basketball player of all time.
2. You can't turn a whore into a housewife.
3. YOU HAVE TO BE IN A CALORIC DEFICIT TO BURN FAT.

How To Put Yourself In A Caloric Deficit

Like I said before, the easiest way to put yourself in a caloric deficit is with your diet. I am going to show you two methods of putting yourself in a caloric deficit. The second one is easy, this is the method I use, and the first one is a lot more difficult.

The Difficult Way To Burn Fat: Counting Calories

The difficult method involves counting calories. I already know from experience that almost NONE of you are going to do this. Don't feel bad because I don't do it either. I've done it in the past, and it wasn't awesome. Yes, counting calories is by far the most effective method of putting yourself in a caloric deficit because it takes all the guesswork out. But it is a pain in the ass, not to mention unsustainable for most people's lifestyles.

I have trained many professional athletes, and none of them meticulously count calories. The only people I know that meticulously count each calorie are pro bodybuilders and fitness competitors. Let me explain to you how they do it. First of all, they prepare all their own meals at home. They use a scale and measuring cups to weigh and measure everything before they cook it. They measure everything including how much oil they use to cook.

Then they pack everything up in tupperware and carry their meals around in a cooler wherever they go. Companies actually make coolers specifically for bodybuilders because bodybuilders have to walk around with all their food and cannot go to a restaurant and eat like a normal person. This is extreme, but it gets them the extreme results that they are looking for.

A lot of people *say* that they "count calories", but I know that they are full of shit. *If you are not weighing out all of your food before you cook/prepare it yourself then you are not counting calories accurately*, you are just guessing. You are lying to yourself if you think every restaurant you eat at will give you any sort of accurate calorie/nutrient breakdown for your order. It does not work like that because the chef is not going to weigh and measure shit for you to tell you exactly how much of everything you are getting. He is also not going to measure the oil he uses to cook your meal and tell you exactly how much he used. Asking him questions like that is an easy way to guarantee that your food is prepared with some *secret ingredients.*

Having that said, the best way to calculate your calorie deficit intake is by using the following equation:

Body weight (measured in pounds) x 10 = fat loss calorie consumption

So, if you weigh 200 pounds and you want to lose weight, then you should multiply 200 by 10 which gives you 2,000 calories per day to eat.

Also, the above is not an exact calculation. It's simply a general guideline for "average people" that aren't on either end of the extremes (overweight or underweight). Depending on your body fat percentage and lifestyle you may have to adjust the equation slightly. Tracking your progress each week is the only sure way to make sure your calories are low enough.

Whatever man, you're not going to do this shit anyway so stop kidding yourself. There's an easier and more practical method. I told you not to read this.

The Easy Way To Burn Fat FAST

I've been a personal trainer and nutritionist for over 10 years, and during all of my reading during that time, the simplest most effective way of burning fat that I've ever come across is a diet plan explained in in greater detail in Tim Ferriss' book, "Four Hour Body".

Here's a brief:

Rule #1: Stay away from "white" carbohydrates

All carbohydrates that are or can be white are thus prohibited, except for within 1.5 hours of having completed a resistance-training workout. Included in this category is bread, rice, cereal, potatoes, pasta, and fried food with breading. If you eliminate eating anything white (cauliflower not included, definitely eat the shit out of some cauliflower), you'll be safe.

Rule #2: Keep it simple and eat the the same few meals over and over again.

Successful dieters, regardless of whether their objective is muscle mass gain or fat loss, eat the same couple of meals over and over again. Mix and match, constructing each meal with one from each of the three following groups:

Proteins:	**Legumes:**	**Vegetables:**
Egg whites with one whole egg for flavor	Lentils	Spinach
Chicken breast or thigh	Black beans	Asparagus
Grass-fed organic beef	Pinto beans	Peas
Pork		Mixed vegetables

Eat as much as you like of the above food items. Just remember: keep it simple. Pick three or four meals and repeatedly eat those. Most restaurants can give you a salad or vegetables in place of french fries or potatoes. Mexican food (a personal favorite) for example, allows you to swap out rice for vegetables, which is most conducive to the "slow carb" diet.

The majority of individuals who go on "low" carb diet programs complain of lower energy and quit, not because these diets won't work, but mainly because they consume insufficient calories. A 1/2 cup of rice is 300 calories, whereas a 1/2 cup of spinach is only 15 calories! Vegetables are not calorically dense, so it is critical that you add legumes for caloric load or eat a TON OF VEGETABLES!

Many people eat 6-8x per day to break up caloric load and prevent body fat gain. I think this is unnecessary and inconvenient. I eat 3 to 4 times per day. It looks like this:

10am – breakfast
1pm – lunch
5pm – smaller second lunch
7:30-9pm – Workout
10pm – dinner

Rule #3: Don't drink calories

Drink massive quantities of water plus unsweetened tea, black coffee, or other no-calorie/low-calorie beverages as you like. Do not drink milk, normal soft drinks, or fruit juice. A glass of wine each evening could actually aids sports recovery and fat-loss. Recent research into resveratrol supports this.

My favorite coffee is one I personally formulated, to act as an appetite suppressor. You can check that out here: Fighter Fuel

http://amzn.to/1OqKXff

Rule #4: CHEAT DAY - once per week

I recommend Sundays as your "Cheat Day". You are permitted to eat anything you want on Sundays, and I go out of my way to eat ice cream, pizza, waffles and all of my other vices in excess.

A cheat day is NECESSARY to lose fat! When you are in a caloric deficit for too many consecutive days, many of your body's hormone levels (Testosterone, Leptin, ect..) start to drop because your body thinks it is starving. Your body drops it's hormone levels in an effort to conserve resources because it thinks it needs to slow everything down (including fat burning) in order to survive the famine (a.k.a. "diet"). When your hormone levels drop your fat loss will come to a screeching halt!

Dramatically spiking your caloric intake once a week will bring your hormones back up to normal levels allowing your body to go back into fat burning mode!

That's right: eating pure crap can help you lose fat. Welcome to never-never land.

I already know what you're thinking "If I eat crazy for a whole day, won't I ruin all the progress that I made? NO... HELL NO.... a resounding NO!!!! You see, ***eating "bad" for one day a week will NOT HURT YOU, the same way that eating "good" one day a week will NOT HELP YOU! It's what you do constantly that counts!*** <— (Tattoo that statement into your brain!)

Here is a video of one of my "Cheat Days" http://bit.ly/24Rt4bs

I talk more about cheat days in my book "*Ultimate Cuts*". I also go over a lot more fat loss techniques such as H.I.I.T cardio, intermittent fasting, carb cycling, etc. But I want to give you some of the basics here as well.

http://amzn.to/1S61qQT

How to "Micro Bulk": Gain Muscle Without Getting Fat

Just like before with cutting I will give you two methods of dieting to build muscle. One will be the difficult one that involves counting calories and the other will be the easy method. The one that I use.

Building Muscle The Difficult Way

If you're going to meticulously track your calories and micronutrients here is a good formula for you:

<u>Body weight (measured in pounds) x 20 = muscle building calorie consumption</u>

This should give you enough calories to build muscle. But if you have an active job, Work out a lot, or participate in a lot of sports then you may need to multiply your bodyweight by as much as 25 to gain muscle. You have to see what works for you.

Once you know how many calories you should be eating, the only question is how much protein? Carbs? Fats? Generally speaking, 1 gram of protein per pound of bodyweight is recommended. Personally, the athletes I have trained over the years have seen better results with 2 grams of protein per pound of bodyweight. A lot of people think that's excessive and it may be for most people. But it works well for the people I have trained.

Now let's be clear, I KNOW you are not going to track your calories or the amount of protein you intake every day. You are not going to measure, weigh, and cook all your food at home and carry it around in Tupperware. That's one easy way to ostracize yourself from the rest of society. Fortunately you're not going to have to walk around with a cooler like a weirdo, because I am going to show you an alternative method.

Eating Big The Easy Way: The Portion Size Method

The easiest way to bulk is using what is called the"Portion Size Method". The portion size method allows you to eat out with friends and live a normal life while still building muscle.

When you see "protein, carb, vegetable, or fruit" it means to eat AT LEAST one portion of each. **A "portion" is the size of your OPEN HAND or CLOSED FIST.**

Sample Meal Plan For Someone Trying To Gain Muscle

7:00 a.m. Protein, Carb/Fruit, Vegetable
9:30 a.m. Protein, Carb/Fruit, Vegetable
12:30 a.m. Protein, Carb/Fruit, Vegetable
2:30 p.m. Protein, Carb/Fruit, Vegetable
5:30 p.m. Protein, Carb/Fruit, Vegetable
7:00 p.m. Protein, Carb/Fruit, Vegetable

Food Choices:

Proteins	**Carbohydrates**	**Vegetables**
Fish	Brown Rice	Broccoli
Chicken	Wild Rice	Snow Peas
Lean Steak	Wheat Pasta	Peppers
Lean Ham	Oatmeal	Lettuce
Tuna	Beans	Eggplant
Salmon	Sweet Potatoes	String Beans
Whole Eggs		Spinach
		Cucumbers

Fruits

Any fruit except fruit that has been canned.

In order to make the "portion size method" work, you HAVE to keep track of everything. Allow me to explain...

Keeping Track Of Everything

In order to make the portion size method work, you HAVE TO keep track of EVERYTHING!

- First you have to write down everything you eat EVERY DAY.
- Write down the TIME you eat everyday.
- Write down all of your workouts.
- Measure your waist line, biceps, chest, arms, thighs, calves, etc... (all body parts) every week. (Weigh yourself once a week).

- Check your progress every week and make changes to your diet and workouts accordingly.

By keeping track of EVERYTHING, you can easily see if you are making progress or not. But more importantly, you will know WHY you are making progress or not!

If you are not making progress, you can look at what you have been eating and make the changes to your diet and workouts accordingly.

If you are not gaining weight, then add a portion of carbohydrates to each meal. Basically, by keeping track of everything you can keep making adjustments based on the progress you are making.

You should also be keeping track of everything while you are cutting as well. That's how you know if you should decrease your caloric intake or not.

<u>Keeping track of everything is probably the most important thing you can do to ensure your success in building muscle or burning fat</u>

I go into more detail in this video--

http://bit.ly/1Q5s3eo

Secret #2 Build Mass Faster With Compound Exercises

"If you love life, don't waste time, for time is what life is made up of."
-Bruce Lee

I'm willing to bet that most of you reading this have wasted many hours in the gym. Big chest muscles don't come from doing flys, statuesque legs don't come from leg extensions and curls, and you will not get a massive back by doing one arm cable rows. Ditch the isolation exercises and start replacing them with compound movements to build quality muscle fast!

It's no secret that compound exercises build muscle mass more efficiently than isolation exercises, but why?

Compound exercises work multiple muscle groups at one time, whereas isolation exercises, work just one. Therefore, ***both your time and effort are maximized by choosing compound exercises over isolation exercises***. This book just paid for itself at least 1000 times over with that last line. Time is our most precious commodity and you will no longer be wasting it away. Will you!?!?

Increased hormonal changes that are fundamental for burning fat as well as building muscles are spurred by compound exercises. Testosterone and growth hormone for instance, are both spiked after just one set of intense squats or deadlifts. Compound exercises are responsible for improved insulin sensitivity (another remarkable change that occurs) due to the depletion of glycogen stores in many muscles at once.

One set of deadlifts will engage practically every muscle in your body. It commands a high-intensity output - crucial for building lean muscle and aiding in fast fat loss.

Heavy pulling (rows, pullups, etc.) and pressing (incline bench, handstand pushups, etc.) movements build impressive arms in ways that forearm or bicep curls alone, never could. A heavy bench press is going to do so much more for your arms than an isolation movement like dumbbell curls.

Isolation exercises do have their place (in the grave...just kidding). However, I believe they should only be a small (if any) part of your workout. You will accomplish your goals and build crazy amounts of muscle faster by consistently performing compound exercises.

Isolation exercises are allowed to crawl out of the grave for two reasons - when you have an injury or muscle imbalance you are trying to work around. The last thing you want to do is take more time to heal than is necessary by re-injuring yourself. So, to work around an injured back, you're not going to be doing deadlifts or bent over rows, but you can do curls or tricep extensions so your arms still get a workout. And as far as that muscle imbalance goes, you can target the underdeveloped muscle by isolating it, while the other muscles are not engaged.

Compound Exercises

A compound exercise includes the work of more than one major muscle group at the same time. Most of the load is taken on by one muscle group and the rest is taken on by the smaller (secondary) muscle groups.

By now you realize that compound exercises are the staples of any great regimen. Here is a complete list of the best compound exercises (in no particular order)--

Bench Press (Flat, Incline, or Decline)
Primary Muscle Group: Chest
Secondary Muscle Groups: Shoulders, Triceps

Military (Shoulder) Press (Barbell, Dumbbells, or Handstand Pushups)
Primary Muscle Group: Shoulders
Secondary Muscle Group: Triceps

Dips
Primary Muscle Group: Chest
Secondary Muscle Groups: Triceps, Shoulders

*Rows**
Primary Muscle Group: Back
Secondary Muscle Group: Biceps

Pull-Ups
Primary Muscle Group: Back
Secondary Muscle Group: Biceps

Deadlifts
Primary Muscle Group: Posterior Chain (Hamstrings, Glutes, Back, etc.)
Secondary Muscle Groups: Much Of Lower Body, Much Of Upper Body

Squats
Primary Muscle Group: Quads
Secondary Muscle Groups: Most Of Lower Body (Glutes/Hamstrings), Lower Back

These are the exercises to stick to in order to maximize your gains. Later, I get into more specifics about how and when to perform these exercises. First, a bit more on isolation exercises.

Isolation Exercises

An isolation exercise includes the work of one major muscle group (by itself), while avoiding any recruitment of secondary muscle groups.

This is a list of some isolation exercises (in no particular order)--

*Flyes** (dumbbell, cable or machine)
Muscle Group Trained: Chest

***Lateral or Front Raises** (dumbbell, cable or machine)
Muscle Group Trained: Shoulders

***Biceps Curls** (barbell, dumbbell, cable or machine)
Muscle Group Trained: Biceps

***Triceps Extensions** (barbell, dumbbell, cable or machine)
Muscle Group Trained: Triceps

***Leg Extensions**
Muscle Group Trained: Quads

***Leg Curls**
Muscle Group Trained: Hamstrings

***Calf Raises**
Muscle Group Trained: Calves

These are exercises you can perform in order to work around an injury or bring any underdeveloped body part up to speed. There are a few other situations in which you would want to perform isolation exercises as well, which I will discuss by more extensively comparing them to compound exercises.

Compound Exercises vs. Isolation Exercises

Further understanding the differences between these types of exercises will allow you to make better decisions and design a routine that complements you most, depending on your unique situation.

In broader terms, we know that compound exercises allow you to engage more muscle groups at once. This makes them the optimal choice as they allow you to increase your load, forcing a faster progression, leading to far better overall results. One is the loneliest number - isolation exercises simply aren't able to carry a significant load capacity due to the fact that they are working *on their own*, meaning slower progression and unimpressive results.

With all of that said, there *are* situations where isolation exercises *can* crawl out of the grave.

Maybe you're sticking to compound exercises and your chest is not growing like you want it to, even though you're benching on the regular. In this case you need to add more volume to the chest during a workout. The problem is that all compound chest exercises involve the use of your shoulders (front deltoid) and triceps which are both smaller and weaker than the chest. Therefore they get tired before the chest gets tired...before the chest gets **worked**!

What I like to do is "pre-exhaust" my chest with an isolation exercise like cable flys so that when I bench my chest becomes exhausted at the same time or sometimes even before my triceps and deltoids.

Here is some elaboration: http://bit.ly/24RsB9q

Another prime reason to not completely discount isolation exercises is because they are practically the only way of training several smaller muscle groups like calves or biceps without putting any additional load on the larger (already exhausted from compound exercises) muscle groups.

No matter if what your goal is, I believe you can and will achieve significant results if you build your workout routine with primarily compound exercises.

Isolation exercises can be performed based on your individual needs but they should be kept to a minimum.

Secret #3: Choosing Intensity Wisely

"If you aren't going all the way, why go at all?"
-Joe Namath

That is the question most people ask themselves. Before you can answer that we need to know what your training intensity is. If you can pick up a baby weight and do a million reps with it, that's called low intensity training. But if you chose a much heavier weight that you can only perform a few reps (with perfect form), that's called high intensity training.

Here are common rep ranges and what those ranges are supposed to equate to:

1-5 Reps Per Set = mostly strength
5-8 Reps Per Set = strength and muscle size equally
8-10 Reps Per Set = muscle size with some strength
10-12 Reps Per Set = muscle size with some endurance
12-15 Reps Per Set = endurance with some muscle size
15-20 Reps Per Set = mostly endurance

Now, according to those numbers and their supposed meaning, if your intensity is where it needs to be to achieve your goal, then it's a good platform to launch from. Does it mean that you can't build strength in the 12-15 range? Absolutely not. But again, it all depends on how intense your workout is and what goal you're trying to accomplish.

Intensity Recommendation For Ultimate Mass

If my assumptions are correct you are reading this because you want to increase your overall size AND strength, which means keeping your workout intensity high and your rep ranges between 3-8. There is not a more specific magic number and it changes depending on the results you are getting (or not getting) as well as your intensity during each particular set. I elaborate on that later.

IMPORTANT!!!

Where a lot of people mess up is at choosing a number based on the guidelines, picking a weight to lift, then they get to eight, and they stop, thinking it was a good set. But you don't want to just pick an arbitrary number. You want to choose a weight where you reach "failure" meaning that performing one more rep (with perfect form) beyond a predetermined number (based on your specific goal) is impossible. When we talk about building strength and recommend doing between one and five reps that means if you've done five, six should be impossible, and if six isnt impossible you need to add more resistance or weight to that exercise. Therefore, don't think of it as, "How many reps should I do?" Think of it as, "What weight should I choose that will make me reach failure within my desired rep range?"

If you're going for strength, pick a weight that will make you hit failure in between one and five reps. Don't just arrive at five reps, think it means something, and set the weights down. "But, I'm feeling the pump man." No, you've got to hit "failure" between one and five reps over and over again to see results over time. Learn to embrace "failure" ...it will get you far in the weight room, and in life.

If you're going for building "Ultimate Mass", you've got to pick a weight that will cause you to hit failure in between six and twelve reps. "Failure" is what's important.

What Does Failure Mean?

I come from the school of thought that you should always go to failure on every set. That's not necessarily old school thought, it's just what I have found to be the best way. Failure to me, is the moment your form is no longer immaculate/perfect. That's when you are done with your set. You have worked the target muscle group to exhaustion.

Picture this, you're doing Killer Carter Curls - which are an isolation exercise - and you're doing great, but then you begin to lean back or swing, and it's definitely not a fucking lower back exercise. Killer Carter Curls are surely bicep curls, not lower back curls. So, the second you lean or swing, you are using your back. That means your bicep can no longer lift the weight by itself. Your back is assisting, aka doing the work which means you're not laser focused and paying attention to your goal, but you are cheating. Now that's what we call a "slut rep" because it is basically worthless and anyone could have done it (and many people do). You are lifting with bad form when you do slut rep. You can catch a form transmitted disease, or an "FTD" that way. FTD's include things like pulled muscles, herniated discs, etc. Strictly do quality reps and once you reach a point where you surely wouldn't be able to brag about it's quality to your mommy's face...when your form is no longer immaculate, that to me is "failure".

http://bit.ly/1sGWE7R

For me personally, if I'm looking to build size, I usually pick a weight that I can only do between 6 and 8 times. If I can do a 9th rep with perfect form, that means I need to increase the weight. If I can't do 9, and I barely get 8 with perfect form, that means I picked the correct weight for my goal. If you don't get to that performance failure, then your muscle will not have a center to grow because it can handle the weight, it can handle the resistance. You've got to give it a little bit more than it can handle so it learns that it needs to be able to handle more. You can let each muscle know that more is required of it. Let your muscles know that their current level of strength is insufficient and you will not tolerate it. Not on your watch. Let your muscles know that you demand more of them. Do that by going to "performance failure" on each and every set.

I explain it more in this video: http://bit.ly/1XXT3iZ

Secret #4: Time Under Tension

"It does not matter how slowly you go so long as you do not stop."
-Confucius

Basic Rep Break Down

Start Position - the place where the weight is held just before movement or engagement of the target muscles into each rep.

Concentric Motion - When you are moving the weight away from the beginning position; moving against the resistance. Also known as the "positive" or "lifting" portion of a rep. Always focus on the target muscles while powering through this motion in a fully controlled manner. I've always liked the expression, "with a sense of urgency", and that's how each concentric part of the rep should be performed, with full control of the weight and with a sense of urgency. This NEVER means to use momentum to move the weight from the starting point to the ending point. It just means, in a controlled fashion where proper form always remains intact and nothing crazy/stupid/funny happens, you should move the weight in a powerful, forceful, swift motion.

End Position - the place where the weight is at the fully contracted part of the rep.

Eccentric Motion - Moving the weight back towards the start position. Also known as the "negative" or "lowering" portion of a rep where you are moving with the resistance. Always remain in full control of the weight during this motion; just think "nice and easy." This NEVER means to drop the weight or let to the weight control the speed of your movement. That is the opposite of control - it's sloppy and means you aren't focused, or that you chose a weight that is way too heavy.

Rep Speed and Time Under Tension

This is something I want to just touch on for those of you that are curious about it. I receive a ton of questions from all over and I've gotten enough about this topic that it was at least worth a mention here. However, I have never trained with or recommended measuring either of these things to a degree that in any way distracts from maintaining total control of the weight and performing each rep with absolutely perfect form.

Rep speed is the tempo (or speed) at which a single rep of an exercise is performed.

Time under tension is basically how long each set lasts. As a general guideline:

1-20 seconds = ideal for strength
20-60 seconds = ideal for muscle growth
60+ seconds = ideal for muscular endurance

Time under tension can obviously fluctuate based on the rep count or the rep speed. But the guidelines exist for a reason, so don't go too crazy. A middle range (6-12 reps) is the most ideal rep range for muscle growth along with a pace that is neither too slow or too fast. If done in a controlled manner and at a speed that seems sane, no matter what you'll be activating the muscles properly. Just make sure your overall workout program is designed specifically for your goal, that you're performing each exercise with perfect form, and that you're workouts get progressively more challenging. As long as you're doing those things right your time under tension will automatically end up being what it should be. And as long as you're avoiding looking fucking "crazy" you're probably doing your reps just fine. What I mean is that both crazy fast and crazy slow speeds need to be avoided.

Like always, there are special considerations to take into account and no recommendations are a "one size fits all" by any means. Certain areas of the body - like calves respond well from moving slower throughout the rep and pausing for a moment at the starting point of each rep. Moving a bit slower can allow for greater control thus helping to prevent/avoid injury - that goes for all exercises.

Secret #5: Rest Times

"Without hard work, nothing grows but weeds."
-Gordon B. Hinckley

There are questions I wish I would never receive, and then there are questions I don't hear enough, which to me, means that people are not giving certain areas proper attention and consideration. I think one of the most overlooked, and under elevated areas of GREAT importance when it comes to working out are timing your rests between your sets and exercises.

You can walk into almost any gym in America and watch almost any dude in there for five minutes and you will notice he is not timing his rest between his sets. He is totally just winging it. After he's done with a set he'll play on his phone or maybe bullshit with his "workout partner" until before you know it the "workout" is over and there was no consistency to much of anything they did especially in regards to timing anything. This is absolutely crazy to me! If you want optimal results, you must track and manage progress. You need to workout smarter so your efforts will be maximized. With that said, it is imperative that you understand and appreciate the importance of timing your rest periods during your workouts. Treat your entire workout like a job, where you have real risks at stake, because you do - mainly your quick/efficient/consistent progress (or lack thereof). A rest or conversation or any other distraction that falls between your set making that time too long or too short, can have negative consequences that impact your results and delay your progress.

Your Goal, "The Dictator"

What are the perfect rest times for you?

Well, what's your main goal? By now this should be clearly defined as it is the biggest factor for shaping your entire routine which you now know - includes timing your rests.

Your workout intensity is another factor that must be considered when choosing the perfect rest times. For best results, lower intensity sets require very little rest between sets.
By contrast, higher intensity/more demanding sets require a longer rest time between sets. This may seem like common knowledge but the lack of or improper application (or sheer neglect) astounds me all the time!

Exercises for bigger muscle groups like legs, chest and back typically need more rest between sets than exercises for smaller muscle groups like biceps, triceps and calves.

Compound exercises usually demand a longer rest between sets than isolation exercises.

Complete Rest Times vs. Incomplete Rest Times

Complete rest - allows you to better maintain your work capacity, as well as maximize strength output and total performance. A more complete recovery enables you to better maintain your strength throughout the entirety of the workout session. Something to note however, is that the body does not receive the same host of metabolic benefits as when subjecting it to a more incomplete rest forcing greater fatigue.

Incomplete rest - shorter in duration, promoting greater muscle fatigue which is responsible for producing higher levels in growth hormone and various other metabolic benefits.
The downside is that you sacrifice nervous system recovery ability meaning you will not see maintained strength like you do with complete rest.

Exact rest times you should allocate are, of course, dictated by your main goal. See below for what you think is best for you:

Rest Time Between Sets: 20-60 seconds
Type of Rest: Incomplete
Best for: Muscular endurance, metabolic or circuit training

Rest Time Between Sets: 1-2 minutes
Type of Rest: Incomplete/Complete
Best for: Building muscle

Rest Time Between Sets: 2-3 minutes
Type of Rest: Complete/Incomplete
Best For: increasing strength, and building muscle

Rest Time Between Sets: 3-5 minutes
Type of Rest: Complete
Best for: Strength and muscular power.

The great thing is that you can reap multiple rewards from choosing the right rest time. I rest for 1-2 minutes or more precisely 90 seconds exactly when I am trying to add mass to my physique. It is wild beyond words that so many gym goers/athletes/fitness people (not to mention those who are not in any of the aforementioned groups) go in without any real or written down plan and do some kind of workout based purely on feelings and what their body is "telling them". Or they have a loose routine written down but are still not timing their rests. I should not have to tell you why this is both inefficient and reckless.

I explain it more in this video: http://bit.ly/1Ua8yOf

Secret #6: Supersets

"Don't mistake activity with achievement."
– John Wooden

A superset is a combination of one exercise performed immediately after another exercise of either the same or opposing muscle groups with no rest in between.

Many bodybuilders such as Dave Draper and Arnold Schwarzenegger have used them with great success for mass building purposes. The same is true of my own training.

Supersets are a fantastic way to get a lot of work done in a very short amount of time. While at first it may be hard for you to use the same amounts of weights that you usually use, your cardiovascular system will get used to the increased workload and then your strength will go back up.

Pairing Two Exercises of the Same Muscle Group

The first way to superset is to do two exercises for the same muscle group back to back. Doing cable curls immediately followed by dumbbell curls is an example of a biceps superset. The drawback to this technique is that you will not be as strong as you usually are on the second exercise. However, this is a great technique to exhaust or rather pre-exhaust a muscle and really isolate it.

Pair Two Exercises of Opposing Muscle Groups

In my opinion, this is the superior way to run your supersets for mass gains. For your superset you would pair opposing muscle groups like chest and back, or biceps with triceps. This allows you to use maximum weights once your body gets used to the increased cardiovascular demands. You could also pair different muscle movements such as shoulders and calves, upper abs and lower abs. When pairing antagonistic exercises, there is no drop of strength whatsoever once your cardiovascular system is well conditioned and this is an excellent way to save time!

Here are the top reasons to superset opposing muscle groups:

Gain Strength And Size

Research shows that a muscle's contractions will be stronger and more powerful if preceded by contractions of its antagonist (opposing) muscle group. For example, when you do a superset of barbell rows followed by bench presses, you'll be stronger on the bench. University of Wisconsin researchers found that subjects experienced up to a 15% increase in quadriceps force production when doing a vertical jump following a six second isometric leg curl which worked the opposing muscle group (hamstrings) immediately beforehand. That's huge!

Lose Body Fat Faster

Super sets have a profound effect on total calories burned both during and after a workout. 35% more calories according to a study from Syracuse University where they had subjects perform supersets compared to when they performed regular sets. A 35% increase goes a long way in terms of extra calories burned in one session let alone adding up all of the sessions over time.

Restore Balance

A complete superset program not only restores balance, but helps the progression of underdeveloped muscle groups that are a waste of time to try to isolate under normal circumstances.

Save Time

Supersets = More sets in less time. Need I say more?

Secret #7: Full Body Workouts

"Doing what needs to be done may not make you happy, but it will make you great."
– George Bernard Shaw

Let's cut the bullshit. Full body workouts are WAY better than splits for building muscle mass.

A split routine is a just a fancy method of organizing your workouts so that certain muscle groups are trained on specific days of the week in interval sort of fashion. A good split routine can be written out many different ways. Here are some examples based on how many days per week you might be training:

Two Day Split:
Monday - Chest/Shoulders/Triceps
Tuesday - Back/Biceps/Legs

Three Day Split:
Monday - Chest/Shoulders/Triceps
Wednesday - Legs
Friday - Back/Biceps

Four Day Split:
Monday and Thursday - Chest/Shoulders/Triceps
Tuesday and Friday - Back/Biceps/Legs

Five Day Split:
Monday - Chest
Tuesday - Legs
Wednesday - Back
Thursday - Shoulders
Friday - Arms

Six Day Split:
Monday and Friday - Chest/Shoulders/Triceps
Tuesday and Saturday - Legs
Wednesday and Sunday - Back/Biceps

But forget that! If your goal is to put on as much mass as possible then FULL BODY workouts are the way to go! Training your entire body, each time you suit up for a workout, is the fastest way for anyone to gain serious muscle mass. Full body training is the way to go because life is short and our days are even shorter so let's save us all the time we can as we gain this MUSCLE MASS.

There are three main factors why full body workouts are superior to isolation exercises when it comes to building mass: exercise selection, hormonal response, and frequency.

The number one reason full body workouts are superior to splits is that split routines inevitably involve more isolation exercises whereas full body routines don't allow for much outside of compound movements. Have I driven this point home enough yet? Are you realizing that for the most effective and noticeable results you want to start regularly performing full body compound exercises? I sure as hell hope so.

Along with choosing the right exercises comes an optimized hormone response including three things that are most responsible for building muscle and burning fat. Research has shown that growth hormone will significantly increase after an intense workout especially when the largest muscle groups are stimulated. Insulin-like growth factor (IGF-1), a powerful anabolic hormone, will also experience a rather large output. Therefore, a full body workout creates a greater ability for your body to increase anabolic hormone production. It's been shown that the amount of muscle mass stimulated in a workout is almost directly proportionate to the amount of testosterone that's released. Workouts that stimulate the most muscles produce the most testosterone. THAT, I have time for.

Assuming you're able to make full recoveries between workouts it's safe to say that a higher training volume leads to faster gains. With full body workouts you could manage hitting all the major muscle groups 3-4 times weekly. That's a huge amount of stimuli! Training more often is the key to building muscle fast. And with the full body workout, keep in mind that you are not breaking down the muscle to a point where you can't work it again the day after tomorrow. If you're doing full body workouts (which you should be), you can do it one on Monday, one on Wednesday, and one on Friday.

Let's say we have two dudes. Dude #1 is the split dude. Dude #2 is the full body dude. Throughout the course of the week, the split dude only does one chest workout a week, and his chest gets 16 sets (4 sets x 4 exercises) of volume per week. But the full body dude's chest gets 24 sets (4 sets x 2 exercises x 3 times per week)! Multiplied by 52 weeks, 832 sets of chest is split dude's total chest volume for the year. Full body guy is getting 1,248 sets in per year. Now obviously, you're not going to work out every week during the year. You're going to take breaks, you're going to have some deload weeks. But you get what I'm saying. Over the course of the year, full body dude is going to get a lot more accomplished than the split guy.

But here's the thing - not only is dude #2 getting more sets, all his sets are full of compound/big body movements. Unless you're gonna be on stage doing competitions, I don't think you really need to be doing isolation movements. I fully believe that if you want to put on muscle mass, then compound movements are the way to go every time. That's why, when people saw my pictures from last year to this year were shocked at the size I've acquired. Well, from then until now all I've been doing are compound exercises. I was doing big body, compound movements exclusively. If I were you, that's how I would choose to make gains as well.

Compound exercises allow each body part to get more reps throughout each week. When people saw the leg workout I've been doing as part of a full body routine, they said, "That's all you do? Two exercises!?" Yes, that's all I need. You have to remember I'm doing that three to four times per week. Think about it in terms of volume per week.

I'm not saying splits are bad. Sometimes it's better to just destroy the muscle. There are no pro bodybuilder that I know of that works exclusively off of a full body routine. I think it's because bodybuilders need to get ridiculous definition and be crazy (unsustainably) lean for shows. But a lot of pro athletes, some of which I've trained, do mostly full body workouts, or they at least do full upper body/full lower body splits. They do compound movements because they don't need to chisel up every muscle like a bodybuilder does for aesthetics. They just need to achieve as much strength and power as they can, as quickly as they can.

I talk about this more in this video: http://bit.ly/1YsB1Eo

Putting It All Together

"What one does is what counts. Not what one had the intention of doing."
– Pablo Picasso

I took the liberty of designing a comprehensive workout program that is going to help you put on slabs of muscle mass as fast as possible.

This is customizable of course, as are all programs (you have to do what works for you) but when putting together your program you have a few options depending on how many days a week you are able to work out, how much time you have, and how fast you recover.

Basic Workout Protocol:

This is the most basic workout protocol available and is very good for beginners:

Day 1: Full body (Chest, shoulders, back, biceps, triceps, abs, legs, calves)
Day 2: Rest
Day 3: Full body (Legs, calves, back, abs, shoulders, chest, biceps, triceps)
Day 4: Rest
Day 5: Full body (Back, chest, legs, triceps, biceps, calves, shoulders, abs)
Day 6: Rest
Day 7: Rest

This is what each full body workout will look like when using the beginner protocol.

Legs: Squats *(4 sets of 8-10 reps)*
Chest & Back (Superset): Bench press/Bent over rows *(4 sets of 8-10 reps)*
Shoulders: Overhead Press *(4 sets of 8-10 reps)*
Biceps & Triceps: (Superset) Curls/Close Grip Bench Press *(4 sets of 8-10 reps)*
Calves: Standing Calf Raises *(4 sets of 8-10 reps)*
Abs: Abdominal Assault Workout

Advanced protocol

I deviate from this program a little bit. I am a more advanced lifter, so I want to get more volume during my workouts. I also want to focus on my abdominal muscles and calves more, so I give them a whole day to themselves. My program looks more like this:

Day 1: Full body (Legs, chest, shoulders, back, biceps, triceps)
Day 2: Abs, calves
Day 3: Full body (Legs, chest, shoulders, back, biceps, triceps)
Day 4: Abs, calves
Day 5: Full body (Legs, chest, shoulders, back, biceps, triceps)
Day 6: Abs, calves
Day 7: Rest

Advanced protocol Exercises

Legs:
Squats *(4 sets of 6-8 reps)*
Deadlifts *(4 sets of 6-8 reps)*

Chest & Back
(Superset): Bench Press/Bent over rows *(4 sets of 6-8 reps)*
(Superset): Chin Ups/Weighted Dips *(4 sets of 6-8 reps)*
Muscle Ups *(4 sets To failure)*

Shoulders:
Overhead Press *(4 sets of 6-8 reps)*
Freestanding Handstand Pushups *(4 sets To failure)*

http://bit.ly/1WNZCUt

Biceps & Triceps:
(Superset): Curls / Close Grip Bench Press *(4 sets of 6-8 reps)*
(Superset): Cable Curls / Cable Tricep Extensions *(4 sets of 6-8 reps)*

Calves:

Standing Calve Raises (*10 Sets of 10 Reps*)

Seated Calve Raises *(4 sets of 6-8 reps)*

Abs:

Dragon Flys *(4 sets To failure)*

Cable Crunch *(4 sets of 6-8 reps)*

Windshield wipers *(4 sets To failure)*

Abdominal Assault Workout

http://bit.ly/1UkiORn

The advanced protocol is probably going to be too much volume for most people. If the beginner program is too basic for you (it is probably not) then you can feel free to add a few exercises from the advanced protocol.

Bonus Chapter #1: Sleep

Most people assume that the only time you build muscle is when you are in the gym, but the truth is that your body mostly build muscle outside of the guy when you are sleeping. In fact, the right sleeping habits offer an easy way to help you burn fat and build muscle mass fast.

Why Sleep is Beneficial for Building Mass/Losing Fat

The Annals of Internal Medicine published a research report which showed that sleep is an important element for weight loss. In the study, it compared two groups of women who were both on calorie restricted diets. One group had 5.5 hours of sleep at night, and the other group had 8.5 hours of sleep at night. The results of the study showed that the group who had more sleep at night lost more fat within a two week period of time. Even more surprising was the fact that the people who slept less at night started to lose muscle mass. A real nightmare if you're anything like me. A lack of sleep causes a shift in metabolism that results in fat preservation and muscle degradation at the same time. Yikes!

One of the reasons for these results was that the sleep deprived group had a change in hormone levels within their body. Sleep deprivation results in an increase in the hormone called "ghrelin," which is the appetite stimulating hormone. Many people assume that they burn more calories when they are awake for a larger percentage of the day, but a lack of sleep actually slows the metabolism so that the body can preserve energy.

Keep in mind that the important step to your muscle building plan is to lose excess fat first! Sleep is a critical factor to help you lose the excess fat stored in the body as well

Why Sleep is Beneficial to Build Muscle Fast

There are several elements that work together to help you develop stronger, bigger muscles. Lifting weights helps you to build muscle because the weights cause small tears in the muscles. But, lifting weights isn't enough, because you also need to provide your body with the tools that are needed to recover after the weight lifting session.

The foods that you eat will impact your muscle growth, because the nutrients are used to repair the muscle tissue. Even if the right nutrients are available, they can't be effectively used until you rest the muscle tissue for awhile. Therefore, sleep is the perfect opportunity for the body to rebuild and repair, and when you close your eyes at night a lot is happening on a cellular level.

Sleep is the primary way that your body can repair muscle damage from your workout, and if you are cutting your sleep hours at night then you are robbing your muscles (and body) of the time that is needed to recover. For optimal muscle building results, you need to make sure that you allow those torn muscles to heal before your next exercise session. If the muscles aren't healed yet, then you will be at a disadvantage.

Also, consider the fact that sleep has a direct impact on your stamina and mental toughness during your exercise session. If you missed a few hours of sleep the previous night, then it is more likely that you will struggle to maintain your regular exercise endurance because you will be tired. People are also more likely to cheat on their diet plan when they are tired, because their body is craving a fast boost of energy from food and their minds aren't as strong to make better decisions..

How Much Sleep Do You Need?

The recommended eight hours of sleep each night is a good goal for average people, although some people find that seven hours per night is sufficient. However, I'm guessing if you're reading this book then YOU are not average or "other people". You may need up to 9 hours for optimal recovery from intense workouts. Listen to your body, and you can adjust the exact amount of sleep to match your individual needs.

Making sleep a high priority is beneficial to so many other aspects of your life as well. If you want to build mass fast, avoid over-training, and prevent fat storage in your body, then you need to make sure that you are getting plenty of sleep each night.

Bonus Chapter #2: Water

"Water is the driving force in nature."
-Leonardo da Vinci

The benefits of water are not to be taken lightly or for granted. I'm willing to bet that almost all of you reading this are not getting enough water on a daily basis. This MUST change if you are to improve your overall health, burn more fat, and build more muscle.

Water Improves Digestion

When you are drinking plenty of water, it helps the digestive system function at an optimal level. Digestion function is a key factor to fat loss and muscle gain, because your body needs to access the nutrients within the food in order to build muscle. If those nutrients aren't readily available, then your progress will slow down because the body won't have the building blocks that are needed for muscle repair. Water helps to improve the digestive system so that your body can break down the food into amino acids, and those amino acids are used to repair muscle tears and help you add mass. Additionally, water consumption can help to optimize your metabolism, which in turn increases your body's fat burning rates.

Water Helps You Feel Satisfied

It has been found that many people commonly mistake thirst for hunger, causing people to reach for a snack when their body really needs a drink. Snacking too frequently can result in fat storage because of the excess calorie consumption and production of ghrelin. On the other hand, controlling your calorie consumption is an effective way to lose fat and slim down.
Water is calorie free, and it helps to fill your stomach so that you can control your portions. Additionally, it helps you to feel more satisfied between meals, helping you to overcome food cravings. Next time you have the urge to reach for a snack, drink a tall glass of water instead. After drinking the water, wait for 20 minutes and then decide if you are still hungry. If you are still experiencing hunger after drinking the water, then you can eat a snack at that point.

Water Detoxifies the Body

One important element for fat loss is to make sure that you are getting rid of the toxins within the body, and some doctors have even suggested that toxins are stored within the fat cells of your body. By drinking plenty of water, you can flush out the waste and help your body to get rid of any toxic compounds. Water stimulates the natural cleansing organs, including the liver, kidneys, colon, and largest organ, your skin. By increasing your water consumption you might experience a "cleansing reaction" initially, because your body is working to get rid of the waste. But, once the waste is flushed out of the body, you will feel even better than usual.

Preventing Injuries with Hydration

Water can help you to prevent injuries, because it lubricates and cushions your joints. One of the worst experiences is to injure yourself during a workout, because it will completely derail your exercise plan. It sucks to be injured! If you're fortunate enough to have avoided injury then hats off to you. If you become injured, it could cause you to miss several weeks of training, resulting in slower progress or no progress during that time. Protecting your joints, muscles, and bones is imperative if you want to build muscle fast, because a healthy body will allow you to stay consistent with your routine.

How Much Water Should You Drink?

Even a small 10-20 percent muscle contraction can cause the body's water levels to drop by as much as four percent. So, make sure that you are drinking plenty of water before, during, and after your workout. We've all heard the recommended, "8 glasses of water every day", but the truth is that everyone is a unique snowflake and their body might require a unique snowflake amount of water. Several factors can impact your need for water, including the types of foods that you are eating, how much time you spend exercising, and other elements of your daily life. People trying to add MASS need much more water than the average person.

Instead of counting the glasses that you drink each day, a better solution is to pay attention to the color of your urine. If your urine is yellow, then it means that you need to increase your water consumption. Darker colors of yellow indicate that you are dehydrated, so try to drink enough water so that you eliminate the yellow color as much as possible. You will likely notice that your urine is yellow first thing in the morning, and that is because you have been sleeping all night and your body is slightly dehydrated when you wake up in the morning. Also, it is common for urine to change color after you have taken supplements, so pay attention to the time that you took the supplements and how it impacts the color of your urine.

BONUS CHAPTER #3 "5 Proven Methods for Gaining Self Discipline"

"We must all suffer one of two things: the pain of discipline or the pain of regret or disappointment."
-Jim Rohn

Let's start with a statistic – 67% of Americans who have gym membership never even use them, that's 2 out of 3 people. Now an average gym membership costs about $58 according to the 2014 statistics and that means Americans are spending more than 6.7 billion dollars every year. 6.7 Billion dollars (for those who are too busy counting the zeros) is more than what 38 countries make a year - and we are spending it just to sit on the fucking couch. Now I'm no expert on the fine arts of couch sitting, but from my experience, I'm pretty sure that you can do that shit for free.

Now why does this happen? I've already talked about seeing a lot of new faces in the gym during the beginning of the year - turns out that is true. It is estimated that gyms get between 30-50% in members in the first week of January and the second week is the busiest week of the year. It's the time of the year when people go- "My New Year's resolution is that I'll **finally** work out regularly this year." Notice that word "**finally**?" They always say **finally** because it's the same fucking resolution they made the previous year and the year before.

Now these guys go to the gym for the first 2 weeks and about 80% will drop off at the end of week 2. There was an actual scientific study carried out about this at Berkley and their conclusion is that it's not because they're lazy; it's because of what they call "hyperbolic discounting" - which basically states that people will pick the option which comes faster. Most people think that results from working out are like cheeseburgers from McDonalds where they'll go "yeah, I'll have a body like that" and expect to get it less than 5 minutes. So when the kid behind the counter goes "Yeah, for that you'll have to work really hard for that and it'll take 4-6 months" most people freak out and don't come back. After all, you won't wait more than an hour for a cheeseburger, will you?

But **you** are not like those people, are you? No, you understand quite clearly that it takes hard work to get that perfect body. Some of you might have heard of Malcolm Gladwell's rule that you can master anything if you practice for 10,000 hours. Hell, if you work hard enough, you can do anything- you've been told this your whole life, right? Just one question- how do you work hard? Because nobody tells you that, do they? They automatically assume that if you want something, you'll work hard for it. And you will, I expect you to work real hard until you reach *your breaking point*, and like everyone who drops out of the gym within 2 weeks will go, *"This is bullshit, fuck this*" when you don't get the result you are looking for.

Now the bad news is - everyone has a breaking point. And that's because we're human beings, not some fucking terminator that can go on forever. What most people don't realize is that we only do the hard work *because* we want to get the result, if we don't get to kill John Connor, we'd probably quit to be the Governor of California as well.

The good news is we can extend our breaking point with self discipline. Those guys who don't quit after 2 weeks of working out are the ones that go, "Okay, this is harder than I thought, but I can still do this". Obviously this becomes harder as you go along (at which point, you should look at other reasons as well) and you'll need more self discipline at this period.

And I'll tell you exactly how you can do that.

Make sure you have the right motivation

Quick, stop reading this article right now and give me 500 squats.

Huh, none of you did what I just said, did you? (Note: to the one guy who did the 500 squats just because I said so, I am promoting you to be my chief minion. Send me a message later and we can talk more about taking over the world)

But the rest of you who didn't listen to me, consider this scenario. You are just reading this book in your room. Suddenly a guy kicks in your bedroom door wearing a ninja mask, a purple T-shirt, hiking boots and no pants; he stinks of cheap vodka and has a butcher knife in one hand and the cutest puppy on earth in the other. And the guy goes, "G*ive me 500 squats right now or I'll cut off the puppy's legs!"*

Now if the guy had said, "*I'll kill the puppy*", that's not a threat, it's just a drunk guy yelling and he probably won't do it (because who the fuck would kill a puppy?). But cutting off the puppy's legs? That's a cold crazy psychopath right there, and I'm guessing he'll do it. And I expect most of you'll probably start doing squats right there. Why? Because you are trying to save a puppy from a psychopath. And for me that's one of the noblest reasons that anyone can give why they are doing squats.

And that is exactly how you should feel like when you do something. *If you are hitting the gym because you thought that it would be a good idea when you were drunk with your friends on New Year's eve, there is no way in hell that you will go through with that.* I got drunk one time and thought that I'd make a great president; do you think Obama is worried about President Brandon? It's the same thing, if you are to follow through with anything, whether to be a great president or a great artist or getting that perfect body, you should really believe it is as important to you as saving that puppy. No matter what that reason is, if you truly believe that it's important, then you have a head start in gaining self discipline.

Setting medium term goals

Now I've already told you about how some people lose it when they don't get any results in the first few weeks or months and quit. The best way to deal this is to set realistic goals.

Let's take the example of school- when you were in your kindergarten, most of you didn't even know your ABC's. If I went back in time and gave the 4 year old you a big ass novel and told you to read, I'd imagine most of you would start crying. But if I did that now, most of you would be able to read it, how did it happen? Well, you learned your letters, then you learned about putting those letters together to form words and then to put those words into sentences. You didn't learn all of this in a week either; you had to pass every grade and it took you more than 10 years to get your ass out of high school.

If you start training from scratch, you won't be seeing much gains right away. But all you have to remember is how much farther you have reached now compared to when you started. You can lift heavier weights now, run faster, your endurance is higher and you can probably kick your beginning-of-training versions ass any day of the week.

Understanding willpower

I've read this really interesting article on the subject of willpower, did you know that you can run out of willpower by the end of the day? Apparently willpower is kind of like your muscles, you can only use it for so long before you lose it. And when you lose your willpower, it really screws with your brain and decision making process-the part of your brain which handles willpower is in the same area where you make short term decisions.

What that means is that your willpower decreases each time you make a decision, and when you are forced to make too many decisions your willpower drops to zero and your brain goes "Fuck this shit, I'm out". This is an actual serious problem- prisoners who are appealing for parole has a 65% chance of getting a parole in the morning compared to zero in the afternoon, regardless of their crimes because the parole officers lose their willpower to make the right decision after hearing for so many cases

So if you are overwhelmed by something, think about what time it is and what happened during the day. Was it one of those completely fucked up days where you feel like the universe just hates you and everything bad happened to you? If that's the case, then good news- your willpower just ran out for the day and the best thing to do is to go to sleep! Sleep helps you to regain your willpower faster and if you really want to make the best decisions, make them in the morning when your brain hasn't had much to think about.

Or in other words, don't trust your stupid fucking brain at night because he's basically drunk at the time, wait till morning.

Remove all temptations/distractions

Let me tell you something about Barack Obama- he is the President of the US, he has to deal with thousands of decisions a day about everything from politics to politics (I don't know much about politics) and still manages to do cardio and weights for 45 minutes a day. Do you know how he does it? Here's a quote from the guy- "<u>I don't want to make decisions about what I'm eating or wearing because I have too many other decisions to make</u>."

And that is how disciplined our President is when he comes to managing his time. There's also this cool observation about Bill Gates- ever since he founded Microsoft, the guy has been making about $2000 per minute. Now if he accidentally drops a hundred dollar bill, Bill Gates is technically losing money if he takes more than 5 seconds to pick it up.

These are two of the most important people in this country right now, where every decision they make means a lot. They literally can't afford to waste their time and they do this by eliminating every single distraction from their lives. And as I said, your willpower decreases with every decision you make, so why waste it on some stupid decisions?

So when you are working or working out it is better to turn off your phone and the Internet. Most of the time, removing the distractions and temptations is a lot easier than trying to use discipline to not use them.

Don't worry if you fuck up

Picture this scenario- you are 8 months old and one day you suddenly started walking. Your parents are so happy to see their kid walking for the first time and everyone is looking at you. Then suddenly you fall down and you go "This is bullshit, fuck walking." Does this sound stupid to you?

Because no, you didn't do that. You fell, cried for a while, tried walking again, got a bit farther and fell again and repeated the same process till you could walk properly. And that is why you are still walking today instead of crawling like a baby.

Why don't we do this in adult life more often? The baby version of us were geniuses in a way, they didn't mind screwing up and always picked themselves up and kept moving forward. And soon they grew into the current version of us who is insecure about making mistakes and worried about making a fool out of themselves. And we are way too quick to go "I can't do this" even before they learned to walk. You have to realize that it's okay to fall down because that's how you learn.

In the video below I go into great detail about how I personally go about building discipline and character in my own life. http://bit.ly/1Q5QZ5H

BONUS CHAPTER #4: "8 Ways To Naturally Increase Testosterone Levels"

"You have to be a man before you can be a gentleman."
–John Wayne

Testosterone is a hormone that is secreted in both men and women. It is responsible for sex drive, as well as protein processing for muscle mass development and strength. The more Testosterone you have, the easier it will be for you to gain muscle and burn fat. Males produce about ten times the amount of testosterone as females do, but females are far more sensitive to its effects. Though testosterone is largely responsible for those traits and characteristics that are considered "masculine" – physical strength, body hair, dominance, and virility – both sexes require it for proper sexual and physical development.

Check our this video of me talking about increasing testosterone naturally-- http://bit.ly/1OqlpOd

8 Ways To Naturally Increase Testosterone Levels

1. Eat More Fat and Cholesterol

Our diet plays a huge role in our testosterone production. Our glands need certain minerals - like zinc and magnesium - to get testosterone production started and our body needs cholesterol to make testosterone.

To boost your testosterone levels you need to increase your fat and cholesterol intake. Studies have suggested that higher fat and cholesterol consumption results in increased levels of total T; men with low-fat diets typically have decreased T levels.

If you're anything like most people on planet earth you're currently thinking, "Isn't cholesterol bad for you?". The short answer is HELL NO!

Cholesterol is GOOD for you! Your body can not make testosterone without it! Your body NEEDS cholesterol to make testosterone!

If you're interested in learning more about the myths and benefits of cholesterol, I highly recommend reading this in-depth, well-written, and well-researched article:

"The Cholesterol Myth That Is Ruining Your Health" by Dr. Joseph Mercola
http://bit.ly/1GOwRxg

I eat at least four WHOLE eggs every night. It is important to do it at night because your body makes most of your testosterone while you are asleep.

Here is a video of me making EGG "MUFFINS"! You need to check this out!
http://bit.ly/1S5ReHZ

2. Eat More Nuts

Your testosterone levels will increase if you eat 20 almonds at least 2 times a day. I can not find the clinical data online about almonds, but I did read in Tim Ferriss's book "The 4 Hour Body" that almonds increase testosterone. Tim recommended eating 20 almonds 4 hours before sex for an extra boost! Because I live in world where I might have sex at any given moment, I am going to be eating 20 almonds at least 3 times a day. HERO MODE!

You will also want to add some brazil nuts. All nuts are little fat bombs that provide the cholesterol that cells need for T production. One study suggest that the selenium in Brazil nuts boosts testosterone. Try eating 3 Brazil Nuts 2-3 times a day.

3. Take a Vitamin D3 Supplement

Vitamin D3 actually isn't a vitamin, it's a hormone - a really important hormone that provides a whole load of health benefits. Our bodies can naturally make vitamin D from the sun, but recent studies have shown that many westerners are vitamin D3 deprived because we're spending less and less time outdoors. When we do decide to venture outside, we slather our bodies with sunscreen, which prevents the sun reaching our skin to kick-off vitamin D3 production. If you're not getting enough sun, you may have a vitamin D3 deficiency, which may contribute to low T levels. If you think you need more vitamin D3, supplement it. Studies have shown that men who take this supplement see a boost in their testosterone levels. Because I have a darker complexion - which makes me prone to Vitamin D3 deficiency - I take 5,000 IU of vitamin D3 in the morning and 5,000 IU before bed for a total of 10,000 IU each day!

4. Take Omega-3 Fish Oil

Fish oil has been shown to improve heart and brain health as well as increase production of the Luteinizing hormone (the hormone responsible for triggering the testes to produce T). Because of the increased amounts of saturated fats and cholesterol you will be consuming, you want to make sure you get enough of the"good" fats to clear the gunk out of your blood.

5. Lift Weights

If you want to increase testosterone, you've got to start lifting – and lifting heavy. Doing circuits with the weight machines won't cut it.

Here's what the research says on how to craft your weightlifting routine to maximize testosterone production:

- Use compound lifts. Squats, bench press, deadlift, and shoulder press should be your main lifts. Exercises that work large muscle groups are associated with higher increases in testosterone.

http://1.usa.gov/1UdFmv8

- **Go for high volume.** Workout volume is determined by the following formula: sets x reps x weight. Studies suggest that higher volume workouts result in higher T production.

http://1.usa.gov/1UdEJSh

Here is a good weight lifting workout you can try-- http://bit.ly/1Uk8Wft

6. HIIT CARDIO Training

You already know how much I LOVE HIIT!!!! So in addition to weightlifting, studies have shown that HIIT workouts can also help boost testosterone levels. For those of you who don't know, HIIT stands for high-intensity interval training. It calls for short, intense bursts of exercise, followed by a less-intense recovery period. You repeat with the intense/less-intense cycle several times throughout the workout. In addition to increasing T, HIIT has been shown to improve athletic conditioning and fat metabolism, as well as increase muscle strength.

If you would like to follow the HIIT training protocol that I personally use, check out Direct HIIT: http://www.directhiit.com/.

7. Get More And Better Sleep

Most Americans today are sleep deprived, which may be a contributing factor to declining testosterone levels in men. See, our body makes nearly all the testosterone it needs for the day while we're sleeping. That increased level of T that we experience at night is one of the reasons we wake up with "morning wood." (If you don't have morning wood on a consistent basis, you might have low T).

If you're not getting enough quality sleep, your body can't produce testosterone as efficiently or effectively. In one study, researchers at the University of Chicago found that young men who slept less than five hours a night for one week had lower testosterone levels than when they were fully rested. The drop was typically 10-15%.

Not only does sleep boost T, but it also helps manage cortisol, a stress hormone that has been shown to wreak havoc on testosterone levels when present in high amounts.

8. Manage Your Stress

When we face stress, our adrenal glands secrete cortisol to prepare our bodies and minds to handle the stressful situation - the primal 'fight or flight' response. In small dosages, cortisol is fine and even useful, but elevated cortisol levels for prolonged periods can do some serious damage to our bodies and minds. One area that seems to take a hit when cortisol is high is our testosterone levels. Several studies have shown a link between cortisol and testosterone. When cortisol levels are high, testosterone levels are low; and when testosterone levels are high, cortisol levels are low.

Knowing about the connection between cortisol and testosterone, you should take the following measures to improve your stress management:

- Meditate for 20 minutes, twice per day.
- When you start to feel stressed, get up and go for a walk.
- Practice deep breathing exercises.

9. Take Ice Baths

Take a 10-12 minute ice bath after hard workouts. One benefit I found in my research was that they could increase testosterone levels. I mentioned a 1993 study done by the Thrombosis Research Institute in England that found increased T levels after taking a cold shower. Sorry, I can not find the study online anymore, but ice baths were also mentioned in Tim Ferriss's book "The 4 Hour Body" as a great way to boost Testosterone and speed up recovery as well as aid in fat loss.

http://amzn.to/1RO1Eio

My good friend Dr. Farhan Khawaja has a GREAT video on how to naturally increase testosterone!

http://bit.ly/24RkBVG

BONUS CHAPTER #5: Best Supplements To Burn Fat FAST

"If you don't have a competitive advantage, don't compete."
-Jack Welch

Not a day goes by without someone stopping me in the gym, on the train, or in the street and asking, "What supplements do you take bro?" I secretly HATE that question because it implies that my physique is the direct result of supplementation, as opposed to my relentless hard work and dedication. Having that said, there are a few supplements that I use to HELP me burn fat and build muscle. Here they are listed below, but remember, they are not magic. They will help you reach your goals faster, but do not think that you can just take supplements and get in GREAT shape with minimal effort. You must do the other things I have outlined in this book first and foremost. Supplements can and do make life a bit easier when they are used correctly, so here are my top recommendations:

FAT BURNER

TEA REXX is the fat burner that I use everyday to stay ripped! A lot of other fat burning supplements make me feel like a crackhead because they have too much caffeine and unnatural ingredients. TEA REXX leaves out substances with dangerous side effects. What it does contain is 100% natural and mainly plant derived. It's even comes in vegetable capsules to avoid consumption of animal byproduct known as gelatin – which is what most other fat burners on the market use.

TEA REXX is safe and effective because it contains natural ingredients:

- Green Tea EGCG
- Green Coffee Bean extract
- Raspberry Ketones
- Ginseng
- Rhodiola Rosea
- Quercetin
- Synephrine

- Yohimbe
- L-Carnitine
- Yerba Mate
- Ginseng
- Rhodiola Rosea
- Moringa Leaf Powder

TEA REXX combines the most concentrated form of green tea extract available with raspberry ketones, green coffee bean, quercetin, L-carnitine, yohimbe, yerba mate, & more. This blend of super antioxidants, herbs, and amino acids gives you a tremendous amount of natural energy as well as fat burning capabilities.

TEA REXX is available HERE: http://amzn.to/1ipVTrr

BCAAs

REVOLT is the supplement I use daily to maintain my hard earned muscle mass. I, as well as millions of other fitness enthusiasts use BCAAs to prevent muscle catabolism. You have likely heard of the term BCAA thrown around in bodybuilding magazines and in supplement ads. Most people, though, have no idea what the term really means.

Muscle is made up of protein, and protein is made up of macromolecules called amino acids. BCAAs are basically the grouping of the amino acids **leucine, isoleucine**, and **valine**. These amino acids are essential because they are not produced naturally by the body and have to be acquired through food or supplementation.

Training on an empty stomach is a bodybuilding inside secret for acquiring maximum fat loss. Unfortunately, training in this manner also depletes you of energy as you are essentially pushing your body without fuel. Not only does this diminish performance but it could also catabolize your muscles.

REVOLT is a supplement designed to help maximize fat loss while preserving every ounce of hard earned muscle. Even if you don't train on an empty stomach, you can still lose muscle through other factors, such as doing too much cardio or consuming an unhealthy diet.

REVOLT is available HERE: http://amzn.to/23fsUvg

PRE-WORKOUT

Right before I perform heavy weight training or HIIT cardio, I use REBELLION pre-workout. Not only is REBELLION the best tasting pre-workout on the market, it is specifically formulated to increase your physical performance and intensity, amplify your muscle pump and endurance, and it helps carry you through amazing workouts.

The secret is a potent, time tested combination of ingredients including creatine, beta alanine, citrulline, betaine, caffeine, and black pepper extract. Each individual is a powerhouse. When combined into one high voltage pre-workout system, they give you the explosive energy, earth shaking power, relentless vigor, and the necessary endurance to help you finally build that rock solid super-hero body you desire.

You can find REBELLION Pre-Workout HERE: http://amzn.to/1UVklKy

COFFEE

If you guys have ever watched a day in the life video of mine or heard me talk about how I start my mornings you know I roll out of bed and go straight to the kitchen for coffee. This has been my routine for years. The problem was that I never really found a coffee that I loved. Some were good, but I wanted something better. That led me to create Fighter Fuel.

Fighter Fuel gives you a more powerful jolt without drastically increasing the caffeine. What most people don't know is that you get more caffeine from a light roast coffee as opposed to a medium or dark roast. Not only is Fighter Fuel a premium extra light roast coffee but it also contains panax ginseng which carries a host of additional vitality benefits.

Fighter Fuel will do more than just give you a slight “buzz” in energy; it will make you feel super charged and ready to train like a mutant on a mission. As mentioned, the energy rush comes from only two ingredients: **Caffeine from a premium extra light roast of 100% Arabica coffee and Panax Ginseng.**

You find out more about and order Fighter Fuel HERE:

http://amzn.to/1OqKXff

Conclusion

"In the end, it's not the years in your life that count. It's the life in your years."
-Abraham Lincoln

Thank you for reading my book. I am positive that if you follow the advice written here, you will be well on your way to getting ripped while gaining muscle faster than you ever thought possible.

I don't want to just sell you a book, I want to see the progress that you have made using everything you have read.

Please keep me updated on your progress! Send me before and after photos, and email me with any questions you may have.

Here are a few ways to contact me:

Fitness Blog http://www.brandoncarter.com/
YouTube http://www.youtube.com/HighLifeWorkout
Facebook https://www.facebook.com/BigBrandonCarter
Twitter https://twitter.com/BCarterMusic
Instagram http://instagram.com/bcartermusic